Menard's Heirs v. Massey

JOHN CATRON

Published in 1850

TABLE OF CONTENTS

MENARD'S HEIRS V. MASSEY

THIS case was brought up, by writ of error, from the Circuit Court of the United States for the District of Missouri.

It was one of those cases arising from a conflict between an old Spanish concession and a title otherwise acquired. The acts of Congress, passed from time to time to regulate these claims, are all set forth in the report of the case of Stoddard v. Chambers, 2 How., 317, and need not be repeated. It is only necessary now to state the respective titles of the plaintiffs and defendant, as exhibited by themselves.

This was an action of ejectment brought by Am ed ee Menard, a citizen of the state of Illinois, as assignee of Pascal L. Cerr e, against the defendant, Samuel Massey, a citizen of the state of Missouri, for the recovery of a piece of land situated in the county of Crawford, and state of Missouri, containing three thousand and one acres and seventy-five hundredths of an acre, being survey number three thousand one hundred and twenty, of three thousand five hundred and twenty-eight arpens of land orginally granted to Pascal L. Cerr e, in township thirty-eight north, of range five west, and townships thirty-seven and thirty-eight north, of range five west, of the fifth principal meridian. This tract of land was confirmed by the act of Congress of the 4th of July, 1836, to Pascal L. Cerr e, the grantee, or his legal representatives, who conveyed to Am ed ee Menard, the plaintiff. Menard died during the pendency of the suit, and his heirs at law were made parties to the suit, all of whom were residents of the state of Illinois. A verdict and judgment were rendered against the plaintiffs in the Circuit Court, the case is brought to this court by the plaintiffs in error.

The case, on each side, as it appears in the transcript, is as follows: On the

5th of November, 1799, one Pascal Leon Cerr e presented his petition to Don Carlos Dehault Delassus, Lieutenant-Governor and Commander-in-Chief of Upper Louisiana, for seven thousand and fifty-six arpens of land, to be taken in two different places, as follows: the half of said quantity, or three thousand five hundred and twenty-eight arpens, to be taken at the place commonly known by the name of the Great Source of the River Maramee; the other half on the head-waters of the Gasconade, and those of the Maramee, known by the name of La Bourbeuse.

On the 8th day of November, 1799, the Lieutenant-Governor, Charles Dehault Delassus, in pursuance of said petition, gave a concession for the quantity of land asked for by the petitioner, reciting that he was well convinced of the facts set forth and stated by the petitioner, and stated further in the grant, that, as it was situated in a desert where there was no settlement, and at a considerable distance from the town of St. Louis, he was not compelled to have it surveyed immediately, 'but as soon as some one settles on said place,' in which case he was required to have it surveyed without delay.

The said Pascal Leon Cerr e, the grantee, produced a letter from Manuel Gayoso de Lemos, Governor-General at New Orleans, to Monsieur Gabriel Cerr e, the father of the petitioner, dated New Orleans, 28th April, 1798, in which he acknowledged the many services which the said Gabriel Cerr e had rendered the government, and his claim to the generosity of the same; and that the said Lieutenant-Governor, seeing the letter of the Governor-General Gayoso, inquired of said Gabriel Cerr e in what manner he might reward him; and that said Cerr e replied, that he was then advanced in years, and had a sufficiency of lands, and recommended his son, who was the head of a family, said Pascal Leon Cerr e, who had then received no grant for any land, to the bounty of the government.

The concession was registered, by order of the Lieutenant-Governor, in the Book of Concession, and presented to the first Board of Commissioners for confirmation, by the grantee, September 15th, 1806; who reported against its confirmation, September 28th, 1810; and the claim was again presented for confirmation, 5th October, 1832, supported by documentary and oral testimony, and was unanimously recommended for confirmation by the Board of Commissioners, October 31st, 1833, and was confirmed by the act of Congress of the 4th of July, 1836, to the said Pascal L. Cerr e, or his legal representatives.

The land as confirmed was surveyed under the authority of the United States, by Deputy-Surveyor Joseph C. Brown, from the 18th to the 20th of June, 1838, under instructions from the surveyor of the public lands in the states of Illinois and Missouri, dated the 6th of June, 1838.

On the 26th of February, 1844, by deed of that date, Pascal L. Cerr e conveyed said lands, as granted, located, and surveyed, to Am ed ee

Menard, under whom the present plaintiffs claim as heirs at law.

By the act of Congress of the 4th of July, 1836, the above decision of the Board of Commissioners, under the acts of 1832 and 1833, was affirmed, and thereby, the title under said grant was confirmed.

The defendant admitted that he was, before and at the time of the commencement of this suit, in possession of the whole of section one, township thirty-seven north, range six west, except the west helf of the southwest quarter of said section, containing eighty acres, which were the same premises on which 'the Big Spring,' at the source of the Maramee, is located.

The heirs at law of Am ed ee Menard, deceased, were admitted, from a statement made by Judge Pope, to be the present plaintiffs.

The plaintiffs gave in evidence a letter from the Secretary of the Treasury of the United States to the Commissioner of the General Land Office, dated 10th June, 1818, in which he was directed and instructed to furnish the receiver and register of the land office at St. Louis, Missouri, with a descriptive list of the land claims which had been presented and registered under the different acts of Congress for confirming the rights of individuals to lands that had not been confirmed, situated within said land district, with instructions to withhold from sale all such lands. until otherwise directed.

The land confirmed to Pascal L. Cerr e, and now sued for, was then within the district of St. Louis. The letter of the Secretary of the Treasury was the official copy, transmitted by the Commissioner of the General Land Office to the register at St. Louis, and was produced by the said register, in whose possession the same was.

The plaintiffs gave in evidence, also, a list of claims which had been made out by Frederic Bates, former recorder of land titles at St. Louis, and which had been presented for confirmation, but not finally acted on by Congress; which list was also produced by the register of the land office at St. Louis, and taken from the files in his office, and on said list was this claim, since confirmed to Pascal L. Cerr e.

Accompanying said list was a certificate made out by Frederic Bates, former recorder of land titles at St. Louis, under date of 10th July, 1818, in which he states,-'The foregoing is a list of claims regularly entered in this office,' and which were supposed to be situated and intended to be located within the county of St. Louis, and which was no doubt made out, in pursuance of the instructions and directions from the Commissioner of the General Land Office, under the direction of the Secretary of the Treasury, reserving said lands from sale.

The plaintiffs also gave in evidence a proclamation of the President of the United States, dated June, 1823, and published in the summer and autumn of 1823, for the sale of public lands, on the third Monday of November in that year, at St. Louis, which were situate in the township and range in which the lands sued for in this action are located, and in which the lands sued for, and contained in the list made out by the recorder of land titles, as above stated, are reserved from sale.

The property in dispute was admitted by the defendant to be worth more than two thousand dollars.

The plaintiffs also proved, by the testimony of Augustus H. Evans, that this claim was located at 'the Big Spring' on the Maramee. And, by the testimony of Henry A. Massey, that, between the years 1826 and 1828, Samuel Massey, in speaking of the works at 'the Big Spring' on the Maramee, said there was an old claim on the land, which he understood had not been allowed, and authorized Major Biddle at that time to try and buy up that old claim.

The plaintiffs also established, by the testimony of Joseph C. Brown, the United States deputy surveyor, that he made the survey of this claim, at 'the Big Spring,' 'as the source of the claim.'

There was offered in evidence, on the part of the plaintiffs, Plat No. 2 from the register's office, and a copy of the original diagram, as certified by F. R. Conway, surveyor of the public lands in the states of Illinois and Missouri, dated Surveyor's Office, St. Louis, 11th April, 1846; which were objected to on the part of the defendant, and the objection sustained by the court; to which decision of the court plaintiffs' counsel excepted.

The above facts, and also a certified survey, under the act of 1836, constitute the title of the plaintiffs in error.

The evidence on the part of the plaintiffs was here closed.

The defendant, as it appears from the transcript, gave in evidence seven patents from the President of the United States, all issued on the 20th of December, 1826, to Samuel Massey and Thomas James, five for eighty acres of land each, and one for eighty-two and ninety-six one hundreths acres, and one other for eighty-one and twelve one hundreths acres of land; and all of said patents covering a part of the same land included in the survey of Pascal L. Cerr e, under the confirmation made to him at the great source of the Maramee.

The evidence on both sides being closed, the counsel for the defendant then prayed the court to direct the jury,

1. That the plaintiffs in this case cannot recover against the defendant for any land embraced within the patents given in evidence by the defendant.

2. That the plaintiffs cannot recover in this case against the defendant, on account of any land within the plaintiffs' survey, without proof that the defendant, at the commencement of this suit, was in possession thereof; and the fact that the defendant had cut wood upon such land is not sufficient to authorize a recovery for the land upon which the wood was cut, if these were merely temporary trespasses and occupation of the land.

These instructions the court gave to the jury; whereupon the counsel for the plaintiffs excepted. and upon this exception the case came up to this court.

It was argued by Mr. Lawrence and Mr. Badger, for the plaintiffs in error, and Mr. Ewing, for the defendant.

The points made by the counsel for the plaintiffs in error were the following:

That the decision made by the Supreme Court of the United States in the case of Stoddard's Heirs v. Harry W. Chambers, 2 How., 284, which is the same in principle as the case now before the court, must govern and settle this case.

That the claim of Pascal L. Cerr e was duly filed with the recorder of land titles, September 15, 1806; and was amongst the first presented to the Board of Commissioners, in accordance with and pursuant to the acts of Congress of 2d March, 1805, and of 21st April, 1806.

The grant was made by Don Carlos Dehault Delassus, who was clothed with ample power for that purpose, as decided in Chouteau's Heirs v. The United States, 9 Pet., 137, and seems to have been prompted by the Governor-General Gayoso himself, from the interest which he took, and the obligations of the government to the father of the grantee for his many valuable services.

The grant called for a special location, but was not required to be surveyed, because of its being remote from the settlements, in the very terms of the concession, and was protected by treaty. It is true, the act of Congress of 2d March, 1805, ch. 86, required all grantees from the Spanish government to file plats, orders of survey, andc. But there was no survey made prior to the confirmation, for, besides not being required by the terms of the grant, in this particular case there was no public officer to do it.

The claim is confirmed, according to the concession, and why it was rejected by the first Board of Commissioners, 28th September, 1810, it is difficult to conceive. The claim had been regularly continued before the commissioners, from the time it was first presented, 15th September, 1806, till it was rejected, 28th September, 1810.

Congress still continued to pass laws to protect the claims which had been thus presented for confirmation. Accordingly, the act of the 15th of February, 1811, provides, 'that, till after the decision of Congress thereon, no tract of land shall be offered for sale, the claim to which has been in due time, and according to law, presented to the recorder of land titles in the District of Louisiana, and filed in his office, for the purpose of being investigated by the commissioners appointed for ascertaining the rights of persons claiming lands in the Territory of Louisiana.' 2 Stat. at L., 621.

The same provisions were extended and continued in force; see 2 Stat. at L., 665, and act of 17th February, 1818 (3 Id., 407); and these claims were again protected by the several acts of Congress of 1826 and 1828, until this claim was finally unanimously recommended for confirmation by the Board of Commissioners acting under the act of Congress of July 9th, 1832, (4 Stat. at L., 565,) providing for the final adjustment of private land claims in Missouri, and, in pursuance of that recommendation, confirmed by the act of July 4th, 1836.

The plaintiffs, therefore, most respectfully contend that the instructions asked for on behalf of the defendant, and given by the Circuit Court of the United States on the trial of this cause, were clearly erroneous. That the patents to Massey and James issued on the 20th December, 1826, could confer no title; for they issued for land reserved from sale, or location, and were therefore void. Wilcox v. Jackson, 13 Pet., 498.

And to bring a case within the second section of the act of 1836, so as to avoid a confirmation, the opposing location must be shown to have been 'under a law of the United States.' Stoddard et al. v. Chambers, 2 How., 317. The sale made, and the issuing these patents to Massey and James, were not made 'under a law of the United States.' They were not only not authorized by law, but were expressly forbidden, and therefore no rights were acquired under these patents.

The counsel for the plaintiffs in error submit, with great respect to the court, that this case is precisely in principle the same as the case of Stoddard's Heirs v. Chambers; and that the decision made in that case by this court will govern in this. That in the one case the owner of land in New Madrid, injured by earthquakes, made a relinquishment of such land to the United States, and, under an act of Congress, received a New Madrid certificate, under which a location was made, and a patent issued in the name of Eustache Peltier, on land covered by a Spanish grant made to Mordecai Bell; and in the other, Massey and James entered in the land office certain lands, and obtained from the government of the United States patents therefor, which lands were covered by a concession previously made to Pascal L. Cerr e by the Spanish government; the lands in both cases being expressly reserved from sale.

And in conclusion they state, that,

1. The plaintiffs in error claim under a confirmation of a grant, protected by treaty, and by the act of Congress.

2. That the decision of the Circuit Court of the United States is erroneous, and ought to be reversed, as being against a title guaranteed by treaty, and protected by legislative enactment. Treaty of 1803 (8 Stat. at L., 202).

Mr. Ewing, for defendant in error.

The claim of the plaintiffs to the land in controversy was submitted under the acts of Congress of July 9th, 1832, and March 2d, 1833, to the recorder and commissioners, and was recommended for confirmation; and it was confirmed by the act of July 4th, 1836, with this saving:

'Sec. 2. And be it further enacted, That if it shall be found that any tract or tracts confirmed as aforesaid, or any part thereof, had been previously located by any person or persons under any law of the United States, or had been surveyed and sold by the United States, this act shall confer no title to such lands, in opposition to the rights acquired by such location or purchase; but the individual or individuals whose claims are hereby confirmed shall be permitted to locate so much thereof as interferes with such location or purchase on any unappropriated land of the United States,' andc.

A part of the land claimed under this concession had been previously surveyed and sold by the United States, and patented to the defendant and Thomas James.

The court instructed the jury that the plaintiff could not recover for any land embraced in the said patents.

1st. The first question is as to the legality of this instruction. The act of 1836 is the grant under which the plaintiffs claim title. It may be right or wrong, just or unjust, but the plaintiffs must take it as it is, and it must be construed altogether, which being done, it amounts to this. The United States confirm to the heirs of Am ed ee Menard all the lands contained in their concession, except so much thereof as has been surveyed and sold, and for that give to them an equal quantity of land elsewhere, to be selected by themselves.

This is the conveyance under which alone the plaintiffs can claim title. They may accept of it or not, as they please, but they cannot make it any thing that it is not.

Out of the statute, if they choose to go out of it for a title, they have nothing on which ejectment can be sustained,-they have no title.

It matters not how strong or how weak may be their right to claim a grant of the very land from the United States. They have got no such grant, and without it they can maintain no action. They are left to their humble petition and remonstrance.

2d. The question arising under the second assignment of error is, whether the action of ejectment can be maintained against a defendant who was not in possession when the suit was brought, and who is not shown to have claimed title, upon evidence that he had at some former period committed trespass upon the land.

It would be difficult to maintain the affirmative of the proposition. Ejectment is a possessory action. Its object is to recover the possession of the property claimed; and, according to the practice in England, the declaration must be served on the defendant, or some one representing him, upon the premises, unless he had left them immediately before to evade service.

It would be confusing the forms of action to allow a recovery in ejectment for a mere trespass, committed at a former period, and unaccompanied with possession, and would involve the absurdity of permitting an individual to maintain an action of ejectment for land of which he was himself in possession at the commencement of his suit.

Mr. Justice CATRON delivered the opinion of the court.

On the 5th of November, 1799, Pascal L. Cerr e petitioned the Lieutenant-Governor of Upper Louisiana for a concession of land, in two parcels, in full property, one half of which, or thirty-five hundred and twenty-eight arpens, to be taken at a place known by the name of the Great Source of the River Maramee, at about three hundred miles from its mouth; the other half, or thirty-five hundred and twenty-eight arpens, at some distance from the first, at the upper part of the headwaters of the Gasconade, and of those of the fork of the Maramee, known by the name of La Bourbeuse, or Muddy. To gratify this petition, the Lieutenant-Governor made the following concession:

'St Louis of Illinois, November 8, 1799.

'Whereas the petitioner is one of the most ancient inhabitants of this country, whose known conduct and personal qualities are recommendable, and being convinced of the truth of what he exposes in his petition, I do grant the petitioner the land which he solicits; and as it is situated in a desert where there is no settlement, and at a considerable distance from this town, he is not compelled to have it surveyed immediately, but as soon as some one settles on said place, in which case he must have it surveyed without delay; and Don Antonio Soulard, Surveyor-General of this Upper Louisiana, will take cognizance of this title for his own intelligence and government in the part which concerns him, so as to enable the interested, after the survey is executed, to solicit the title in due form from the Intendant-General of these provinces of Louisiana.

'CARLOS DEHAULT DELASSUS.'

'Registered by order of the Lieutenant-Governor, pages 15 and 16 of Book No. I., Titles of Concessions.-SOULARD.'

This claim was laid before the first board in the following form:

'September 15, 1806. Pascal L. Cerr e, claiming a tract of a league square, to be surveyed in two parts or halves, the one on the Big Spring of the River Maramee, so as to include said spring, and the other at the fall of the forks of the Gasconade and those of the Maramee, called the Muddy, produces a concession from Charles Dehault Delassus, dated 8th November, 1779.'

That board (September 28, 1810) were of opinion, that the claim ought not to be confirmed; and so reported to Congress. And thus the claim stood until October 31, 1833, when it was presented to the second board, created by the act of 1832; and this board was of opinion, and reported to Congress, 'that the claim ought to be confirmed to Pascal L. Cerr e, or his legal representatives, according to the concession.' And by the act of July 4, 1836, Congress confirmed the claim according to the report, and consequently according to the unsurveyed concession.

The township, including 'the Big Spring of the River Maramee,' was offered for sale on the third Monday of November, 1823, pursuant to the proclamation of the President. Whether Massey and James purchased at the public sale in 1823, or entered afterwards, does not appear from the record; but in 1826 and 1827 they obtained their different patents for the land in dispute, from the United States; and these titles, the court below charged the jury, were superior to Cerre's confirmed claim. And here the question arises, whether Cerre's concession, on being confirmed by Congress in 1836, related back to its date of 1799, and overreached the United States title made to Massey and James. If it does so relate to the extent of the survey made under the confirmation in 1838, and approved in 1840, then the controversy is at an end; and as on this assumption the suit was brought, it becomes necessary to examine the question of relation of title. The argument is, that the concession was made by an officer who and power to grant; and having done so, the land granted was 'property.' and protected by the third article of the treaty of 1803, which declares that the inhabitants of the ceded territory shall be maintained and protected in the free enjoyment of their liberty and property; and that the laws of nations, equally with the stipulations of the treaty, secured the title of such grantees.

That the Lieutenant-Governor of Upper Louisiana had the authority, as a sub-delegate, under the Intendant-General of the provinces of Upper and Lower Louisiana and Florida, to make concessions, is undeniable; he could and did deal with the public domain of the province,-made concessions, directed the lands to be surveyed, and caused grantees to be put into possession. This, however, does not settle the question. It does not depend upon the existence of power, or want of power, in the Lieutenant-Governor, but on the force and effect of the right his concession conferred. Did it give such a vested title in the soil, as that the Spanish government could not legally disavow it? Or could the Intendant-General, representing the royal authority, lawfully refuse to confirm the concession, and order the grantee to be turned out of possession? If it be true, that the title ended with the concession, survey, and occupancy of the land granted, then it follows, that the title was completed and perfected under the Spanish laws, by these acts; nor was a confirmation from any higher power than the Lieutenant-Governor at all necessary; the grantee having all the title that the king could give. The assumption, that such was the Lieutenant-Governor's power, and the force and effect of the title, sets out with the assertion, that neither the regulations of Morales, nor any previous regulation of the Spanish governors, were ever in force in Upper Louisiana, and that the act of the Lieutenant-Governor was conclusive as to law and fact when making grants; that he could grant to any one, for any quantity, and for any reason, or without reasons, and on any condition, or without conditions; and that no authority existed to supervise his acts; and we are referred to various expressions and conjectures on this subject. In the cases of Soulard and Smith T., against the United States, (4 Pet.,) this court, after holding the cases under advisement for a year, professed itself unable, from want of information, to give any opinion in the matter; and, for this reason, the cases were not then decided. This occurred in 1830. In 1835 and 1836, in the cases of Clarke, Delassus, and two of Chouteau's Heirs, found in 8 and 9 Pet., regulations for the government of sub-delegates are admitted to have existed, but not to such an extent as to control the Lieutenant-Governors in regard to person, quantity, or reason, when making concessions and orders of survey; and such has been the doctrine of this court since that time, so far as concessions made in Upper Louisiana have been adjudged. These cases address themselves to a single consideration; that is to say, whether the Lieutenant-Governor's powers were so limited that the concessions then before the court were void for want of power; but they do not settle the question, that the grant was a perfect title. It is said by the court in the case of Chouteau's Heirs, 9 Pet., 154,-'It is remarkable, that, if we may trust the best information we have on the subject, neither the Governor nor the Intendant-General has ever refused to perfect an incomplete title granted by a deputy-governor or sub-delegate.' In point of fact, this is certainly true. No such refusals could take place. From the parts of Upper Louisiana, where grants were made, to New Orleans, where the Intendant-General and Governor-in-chief resided and kept their offices, the distances were so great, and the trackless wilderness between so infested with hostile Indian tribes, that few could apply, had they possessed the means to pay for perfecting their titles. And, in the next place, the principal standard of value was skins in the upper province; specie was hardly known there. And, then, again, land was of no material value to such a population, who resided in villages, and cultivated patches within a common fence, where each inhabitant had his portion assigned by a syndic. But two instances are known to exist in Upper Louisiana, where the Intendant was applied to for a complete title, and made the same; one case was that of Moses Austin for a league square at Mine a Breton, a report on which is found in 2 American State Papers, 678, and the other perfected title was made to Mr. Reigh, in the neighborhood of St. Louis.

The fact, therefore, that the intendant-generals and governors did not refuse to make perfect titles, is no evidence that they had not the power to deal absolutely with concessions made by sub-delegates, and to give titles or refuse them, as the Congress of the United States has done. Like Congress, they exercised the sovereign power. The concession before us addresses itself to the Intendant-General and refers the grantee to him, 'to solicit the title in due form,' as do, uniformly, all the concessions and orders of survey made by lieutenant-governors, after the Intendant was restored to power.

By the eighty-first article of the royal ordinance providing for Intendants of New Spain, (2 White's Recop., 69, 71,) such Intendants were made the peculiar judges of causes and questions arising in their respective districts, relating to the sale, distribution, and grant of royal lands; and, a dispute having arisen in 1797, between Morales, Intendant ad interim, and Don G. de Lemos, Governor of Louisiana, respecting the exclusive right claimed by the former to control such grants, (see Id., 469, et seq.,) the royal order of 22d October, 1798, was issued, reaffirming this eighty-first article, and declaring the powers of the Intendant to be plenary, and in conclusion of all other authority, to divide and grant all kinds of lands belonging to the crown. (Id., 245, 477.) Acting under and by virtue of these two royal orders, the Intendant, Morales, on the 17th of July, 1799, published his regulations, addressed to the lieutenant-governors, sub-delegates, and to the people of the provinces of Lower and Upper Louisiana, and West Florida, so that those who wished to obtain lands might know in what manner to ask for them, and on what conditions they could be granted and sold:'And especially,' in his own language, 'that those who are in possession without the necessary titles may know the steps they ought to take to come to an adjustment; that the commandants and sub-delegates of the intendancy may be informed of what they ought to observe. He then states, that a great number of those who have asked for land think themselves the legal owners of it; those who have obtained the first degree, by which a surveyor is ordered to measure and put them in possession; others, after a survey has been made, have neglected to ask for 'a title to the property;' and as like abuses, continuing for a longer time, will augment the confusion and disorder which will necessarily result, 'we declare, that no one of those who have obtained said decrees, notwithstanding in virtue of them the survey has taken place, and that they have been put in possession, can be regarded as owners of the land, until their real titles are delivered completed, with all the formalities before recited.' The foregoing is an extract from the eighteenth article of the regulations of July, 1799, which regulations had the force of written law up to the time when a change of government took place. The formalities for completing a real title are prescribed by the three articles preceding the eighteenth; the surveyor was bound to forward to the Intendant a survey, and also a copy of the survey, or rather a figurative plot, and a certificate called a procesverbal, signed by the commandant, or a syndic and two neighbors, together with the surveyor, declaring that the survey was made in their presence, and corresponded with the facts stated in the proces-verbal, and on the concession, this figurative plot, and the proces-verbal, the complete title was founded; a copy of the plot and proces-verbal being attached; and which evidence of title was recorded in several departments. Such, in substance, was the real title completed. The necessity of a further title than a mere loose order of survey, given by commandants of posts and lieutenant-governors, and placed in the hands of the interested party, is too manifest for comment. Petitions were written by the party asking the land, or some one for him; the governor consented, usually by indorsement on the petition, and ordered that the petitioner should have the land, and directed that it should be surveyed; the paper was handed to the petitioner, who might deliver it to the surveyor, or omit it; if he presented it, and the land was laid off, then it was the surveyor's duty to record both the concession and plat, together with the proces-verbal. But this did not make the party owner; without the further act of the king's deputy,-the Intendant-General,-the title still continued in the crown.

As assumed in argument, (and truly,) by the third article of the treaty by which Louisiana was acquired, and by the laws of nations, the inhabitants of the ceded territory were entitled to be maintained and protected in the free enjoyment of their property. But in what property? To such an interest in it, if land, as they had when the country changed owners; and that interest being of a character requiring royal sanction before the Spanish government would recognize it as divesting the public title, our government, as the successor of Spain to the public lands, gave the same construction and effect to concessions and orders of survey; holding, that the title of the king's domain passed by treaty to the United States, notwithstanding the existence of such concessions. Yet, to the full extent of any equity in the claimants, the government adopted means to satisfy the claims; and, as the sovereign power could not be sued as legal owner, Boards of Commissioners were created, with liberal powers, to investigate every description of claims, and report on them to Congress, for the sanction of sovereign authority; and by this means many claims were confirmed, the legal title added, and incipient concessions completed into perfect and conclusive titles against the government. Then, again, Congress provided that special courts should be organized, in which the government might be sued, in a prescribed form, and decrees be made for or against claimants; but no suit could be maintained in an ordinary action of ejectment, or for title of any kind, on a concession and an order of survey, for want of legal title to sustain it. Such claimants 'were not regarded as owners of land, until the real title was delivered completed,' in the language of the Spanish regulation No. 18. Had the courts of justice been allowed to hold otherwise, and to interfere in the matter, and to decree titles to claimants in equity, or to enforce their claims at law, and oust the United States indirectly by suing persons found on the land, little or no occasion would have existed for boards, or special courts, to adjudge respecting the validity of claims; as the ordinary tribunals could have settled all controversies under state laws declaring such claims cognizable in the state courts. It was therefore manifest, that claims resting on the first incipient steps must depend for their sanction and completion upon the sovereign power; and to this course claimants had no just cause to object, as their condition was the same under the Spanish government. No standing, therefore, in an ordinary judicial tribunal has ever been allowed to these claims, until Congress has confirmed them and vested the legal title in the claimant. Such, undoubtedly, is the doctrine assumed by our legislation. To go no further, the act of May 26th, 1824, allowing claimants a right to present their claims in a court of justice, pronounces on their true character. It declares, that the claim presented for adjudication must be such a one as might have been perfected into a complete title under and in conformity to the laws, usages, and customs of the government under which the same originated, had the sovereignty of the country not been transferred to the United States; and, by the sixth section, when a decree is had favorable to the claim, a survey of the land shall be ordered, and a patent shall issue therefor; and by section eleventh, 'if the decree shall be in the claimant's favor, and the land has been sold by the United States, or otherwise disposed of, the interested party shall be allowed to enter an equal quantity of land elsewhere.' So, again, the act of July 9th, 1832, creating the last board, directs the commissioners to inquire into and examine all unconfirmed claims previously filed, founded on any incomplete grant, concession, warrant, or order of survey, issued by the authority of France or Spain, and to class the same so as to show, first, what claims, in their opinion, would in fact have been confirmed according to the laws, usages, and customs of the Spanish government and the practice of the Spanish authorities under them 'at New Orleans,' if the government under which said claims originated had continued in Missouri; and, secondly, what claims, in their opinion, are destitute of merit under such laws, usages, and customs. And by section third it is declared, that from and after the final report of the commissioners, the lands of the second class shall be subject to sale, the same as other public lands; and that those of the first class shall continue to be reserved from sale, as heretofore. From the first act, passed in 1805, up to the present time, Congress has never allowed to these claims any standing other than that of mere orders of survey and promises to give title; and which promises addressed themselves to the sovereign power in its political and legislative capacity, and which must act, before the courts of justice could interfere and protect the claim. And so this court has uniformly held. The title of Cerre having no standing in court before it was confirmed, it must of necessity take date from the confirmation, and cannot relate back so as to overreach the patents made in 1826 and 1827.

The next ground relied on to reverse the decision of the Circuit Court is, that Cerre's claim was reserved from entry and grant by the act of March 3d, 1811, providing for the sale of public lands and the final adjustment of land claims. The fifth section declares that back lands to front grants on the Mississippi River, andc., are reserved from sale; and by section sixth it is provided, that, until after the decision of Congress thereon, no tract of land shall be offered for sale, the claim to which has been, in due time, and according to law, presented to the register of the land office for the purpose of being investigated by the commissioners appointed for ascertaining the rights of persons claiming lands in the territory of Orleans. The eighth section declares, that the Surveyor-General shall cause such lands in the Louisiana territory as the President shall direct to be surveyed, like other public lands; offices are established for their disposal, and it is directed that they shall be sold by order of the President. But from this power to sell are excepted section number sixteen, salt springs, and lead mines, with such lands adjoining thereto as the President shall direct; and then comes the exception relied on for the protection of Cerre's claim, to wit,-'That, till after the decision of Congress thereon, no tract of land shall be offered for sale, the claim to which has been, in due time, and according to law, presented to the recorder of land titles in the District of Louisiana, and filed in his office, for the purpose of being investigated by the commissioners appointed for ascertaining the rights of persons claiming lands in the territory of Louisiana.' (See Land Laws, 194.)

That this provision is an exception to the general powers conferred on the officers to sell, is not an open question; having been so adjudged by this court in the case of Stoddard's Heirs v. Chambers, reported in 2 Howard; and again at the present term, in the case of Bissell v. Penrose, post, p. *317. Nor is it an open question, that the act of February 17, 1818, § 3, re-enacts and continues in force the exception as respects such lands. This was also decided by the above cases; and that such was the opinion of Congress is manifest from the third section of the act of July 9, 1832, under which the last board acted; for it declares, that lands of the first class shall be reserved from sale 'as heretofore.' [6]

All these acts of Congress, with their exceptions, address themselves especially to the Department of Public Lands, as by them that department must be guided. In reserving lands from sale, it was necessary to know where they were situated, and how far they interfered with the public surveys. Either the President, or some other officer, must have had the power to designate the lands as those adjoining to salt springs and lead mines; or it must have appeared in some public office appertaining to the Land Department what the boundaries of reserved lands were; and if it did not appear, no notice of the claim could be taken by the surveyors, nor by the registers and receivers when making sales. This was a conclusion that has from necessity been acted on at the land offices; and as Cerre's claim was not surveyed before the confirmation took place, no boundaries of his tract could be recognized when the public surveys were made and the lands sold. He claimed no 'tract of land.' The laws refer to specific tracts that are claimed; it is not material whether the boundaries are proper, and according to the concession, or the claim be just or otherwise, so that the tract claimed be certain. This was also decided in the cases just cited. Certainly, a mere floating claim, founded on a concession that was ordered to be located by survey, and where no survey or location had been made, was not protected by the act of 1811. An actual survey is not indispensable; but boundaries must appear, in some form, from the notice of claim and the accompanying evidences filed with the recorder. If, from these, the tracts could not be laid down on the township surveys, then the land could not be reserved from sale; although, by the concession, and by the notice, a particular spot, (as the Big Spring of the Maramee,) was referred to in general terms as the place where the land should lie.

But there is another ground of defence, that would have been conclusive, even had Cerre's claim been surveyed and the survey filed with the recorder in 1806, accompanying the notice of claim. By the second section of the confirming act of July 4th, 1836, it is provided, that, 'if it shall be found that any tract confirmed by this act, or any part thereof, had been surveyed and sold by the United States, this act shall confer no title to such lands, in opposition to the rights acquired by such location or purchase; and the party whose claim is confirmed by this act shall be authorized to enter a quantity of land equal to the interference elsewhere.'

Having seen that the United States might confirm the claim of Cerre, or might refuse to do so; and that it took date as a title recognized in the judicial tribunals from the confirming act, it follows that the claim might be confirmed in such part, and on such conditions as Congress saw proper to prescribe; and having refused to confirm it for lands lying within its boundaries which had been previously sold, and the patents to Massey and James being of this description, they are the only legal title to the land; and, therefore, the charge of the Circuit Court was proper.

The survey of Cerre's tract, founded on the confirmation, was given in evidence, and recognized as part of his title by the Circuit Court; which circumstance we deem it proper not to pass without notice. By the act of April 26th, 1816, it was provided that a surveyor should be appointed of the public lands for the territories of Illinois and Missouri, whose duty it should be to cause so much of the lands in said territories as the President should direct, to be surveyed and divided as were the public lands lying northwest of the river Ohio; and the act declares that 'it shall also be the duty of the surveyor to cause to be surveyed the lands in said territories, the claims to which have been, or hereafter may be, confirmed by any act of Congress, which have not already been surveyed according to law; and he shall transmit to the registers of the land offices in said territories, general and particular plats of all the lands surveyed or to be surveyed, and shall also forward copies of said plats to the Commissioner of the General Land Office; and all the plats of surveys, and all other papers and documents pertaining, or which did pertain, to the office of Surveyor-General under the Spanish government within the limits of the territory of Missouri, andc., shall be delivered to the surveyor appointed under this act.' 'And any plat of survey, duly certified by said surveyor, shall be admitted as evidence in any of the courts of the United States, or the territories thereof.' Under this authority, Cerre's claim was surveyed; as will better appear by the following certificate, preceding the description of the lines:

'Plat and description of the survey of a tract of 3,528 French arpens, equal to 3,001 and twenty-five hundredths English acres of land, situated in township thirty-eight north, range five west; and townships thirty-seven and thirty-eight north of the base line, range six west of the fifth principal meridian, in the state of Missouri; executed from the 18th to the 20th of June, 1838, by Joseph C. Brown, deputy surveyor, under instructions from the surveyor of the public lands in the states of Illinois and Missouri, dated the 6th of June, 1838; it being the one half of 7,056 arpens, or a league square, granted in two tracts of equal quantity, on the 8th of November, 1799, to Pascal L. Cerr e, by Zenon Trudeau, Lieutenant-Governor of the Spanish province of Upper Louisiana; this tract 'to be taken at the place commonly known by the name of the Great Source of the River Maramee, at about three hundred miles from its mouth, so as to include the said sources;' and confirmed to Pascal L. Cerr e by the act of Congress of the United States approved on the 4th of July, 1836, entitled, 'An act confirming claims to land in the state of Missouri, and for other purposes,' according to the decision No. 2 of the report of the Board of Commissioners appointed by the act of Congress, approved on the 9th of July, 1832, entitled, 'An act for the final adjustment of private land claims in Missouri,' and the act of Congress approved the 2d of March, 1833, supplemental thereto.'

The Surveyor-General approved the survey, June 26, 1840. In having the land laid off, and in approving the survey, he acted under the authority of Congress, expressly conferred by the act of 1816. Joseph C. Brown testified that he made this survey, being the same offered in evidence above; that the survey was made at the time stated on its face, and was made by the witness at the place known and called 'the Big Spring of the Maramee;' that the said spring was on section one, as marked and designated on the plat before him. The Big Spring was a very large body of water breaking out of a high bluff, and made a stream from the spring itself of about one hundred feet wide, and a foot in depth; that witness made the survey by direction, and under the authority given to him by the Surveyor-General of the United States at St. Louis. Witness further stated that the survey was made according to Mr. Cerre's directions, and in obedience to the instructions given to him by the Surveyor-General; Mr. Cerr e made no particular reconnoissance of the ground, although personally present, but took the land as it came; and it was made by the surveyor at the particular place indicated, the Big Spring, as the source of his claim. Witness stated further, that the instructions from the Surveyor-General were printed instructions, of which a copy is set out. Among numerous and detailed instructions referred to by the witness, there are the following:

'Information given to you by a claimant or his agent relating to the situation of a claim will govern your operations, provided you believe, from all the circumstances which come to your knowledge, that such information is correct; and provided also that it does not contradict the papers with which you may be furnished. The position of any point or place called for in a concession, and also of the settlement or improvement in virtue of which a settlement claim is confirmed, must be stated in your field notes. The survey of claims which are confirmed unconditionally, according to a former survey, will conform thereto, regardless of any excess or deficiency in quantity, provided the old lines and corners can be found and properly identified; in which event, the old corners will be run to, and the true courses and lengths of the several lines, according to your operations, will be correctly stated in your field notes; and if the old lines and corners cannot all be found, you will conform to the old survey, as near as practicable, by running the courses and distances called for, or to the intersection of the proper lines, as may be required, making the necessary allowance for the difference in the variation of the needle.

'2. The resurveys of claims which are confirmed according to an old survey, but are restricted in quantity, will be surveyed as above directed for those not restricted, except that, if there is any excess or deficiency, it will be thrown off or taken in a line parallel to that old line of the survey, which the claimant may direct; or if he fails or declines to give directions, throw off the excess or take in the deficient quantity on the side which you think will best promote his interest, being careful to note all the particulars relating thereto in your field book, and give the position of the old lines and corners which may be abandoned because of the excess or deficiency in quantity.

'3. Claims which are confirmed according to the concession, and have been legally surveyed in conformity therewith, except as to exactness in quantity, will be resurveyed as the class of cases last above mentioned.

'4. If the survey heretofore executed of a claim which is confirmed according to a concession, whether the concession is, or is not, special as to locality, but is special as to the direction of the lines, the proportional length of the different sides, or the figure of the survey to be made in virtue thereof, does not conform to these requirements of the concession, the said survey will be altogether disregarded, except so far as it may be useful, in cases where the concession is not special as to locality, in identifying the situation of the intended concession to be confirmed, unless the survey was executed and approved by the proper Spanish officer prior to the transfer of the country to the United States; in which event, the survey will be considered as evidence of the changed intention of the authority making the concession, and will be taken as a part and parcel thereof.

'5. Claims which are confirmed according to special concessions, and which have not been surveyed, you will survey in strict accordance with the terms of the concessions; always bearing in mind, that where there are no special requirements in the concession, it was the general practice of the government with which the claims originated to run them either in squares, or in right-angled parallelograms of one, five, ten, or some intermediate or greater number of arpens, by forty or eighty, according to the size of the tract, or double as long as wide, unless some other survey or grant intervened and rendered a departure from this rule unavoidable; in which case, the rule was only so far departed from as was necessary to get rid of the interference with prior surveys.'

Cerre's claim was of the last class. The land was directed to be surveyed according to his directions; the surveyor having regard to the last (and fifth) instruction, with the exception, that the special spot called for in the concession was required to be laid down and noted in some part of the survey. When it was made, and the field notes returned to the Surveyor-General's office, and the description and plat made out in form and approved by the Surveyor-General, it was conclusive evidence, as against the United States, that the land granted by the confirmation of Congress was the same described and bounded by the survey; unless an appeal was taken by either party, or an opposing claimant, to the Commissioner of the General Land Office. This consideration depends on the fact, that the claimant and the United States were parties to the selection of the land; for, as they agreed to the survey, they are mutually bound and respectively estopped by it. But private claimants of lands within its boundaries, who were no parties to the survey, are not estopped, and may controvert its conclusiveness, so far as their claims interfere with the lands thus selected by the party, and which were laid off to him by the United States. We are not called upon to say, nor do we wish to be understood as intimating, to what retrospective date the confirmation by Congress of land thus surveyed relates, so as to overreach a claim by purchase from the United States, further than the case before us requires, which is, that lands purchased before the act of July 4th, 1836, was passed, are protected against the confirmation made by that act.

For the reasons stated, we order the judgment of the Circuit Court to be affirmed.

For a more perfect understanding of the manner in which a complete title under the Spanish government was executed, the form of such a title, translated from the Spanish, is hereto annexed. [7]

Don Joan Ventura Morales, Principal Comptroller of the Armies, Intendant ad interim of the Royal Finances of the Provinces of Louisiana and West Florida, Superintendent, Sub-delegate, Judge of the Admiralty, of the Royal Lands and Domain, and c.:

Whereas (D. M. D.) an officer of the militia, residing in this city, has appeared before this tribunal, petitioning the grant and title of one hundred and twenty-six arpens of land, with that front to the Bayou de los Lobos and the depth of forty, bounded by (Don F. S.) and vacant lands on the Bay St. Louis, provided they be of the royal domains, to establish there a plantation and cow-pens, stating that he has taken the proper steps and showing that he has made the necessary provisions for establishments of that kind; and having presented the plat of the royal surveyor (Don C. T.), indicative and figurative of the said one hundred and twenty-six arpens in front by forty in depth situated in the above-mentioned place; and having submitted the whole to the fiscal of the royal finances, and he having made no objection to the demand of the said (D. M. D.) but, on the contrary, having given an opinion in his favor, by an act, with the advice of his assessor, dated the 26th instant; I have conceded the said grant, and I do order that the title be made. Accordingly, using the power given to this intendancy, in the name of the king our lord, (whom God protect!) I do grant to the above-said (D. M. D.) the above-mentioned tract of land, containing one hundred and twenty-six arpens in front and forty in depth, situated at the place called the Bay St. Louis, fronting to the Bayou de los Lobos, and bounded by the lands of (Don F.S.) and vacant lands, in conformity to the points and distances marked on the plat and its certificate, in which is recited the measure appearing in the docket of said matter for record; out of good-will, and without any pecuniary consideration in favor of the royal financier, I give him the whole and direct ownership to the said granted land, for him and his successors in said lands, with power to him, the said grantee, to dispose of the same at his will; with power to take possession of the same, and claim it from this intendancy if there is any obstacle; and in said land forthwith I place and put him without any damage to the rights of third persons who may have a better right to it; with the qualification and condition that he, the said (D. M. D.), to whom we do this favor, and his successors, shall, as regards such tract of land, fulfil the obligations imposed upon him by the regulations and instructions made and published by this intendancy on the 17th of July, 1799, to wit, the third, fourth, sixth, seventh, and ninth of said instructions, conformably to the location, place, quality, and circumstances of the said granted land; whereof we advise him, that he may know it and not pretend to be ignorant of it, under the penalties contemplated in said instructions, with which he shall acquaint himself. In virtue of which I have ordered these presents to be drawn under my hand, and sealed with the seal of my arms, and countersigned by the undersigned notary of the royal finances; who, as well as the principal Comptroller's office, will register it.

Given at New Orleans, the 29th of May, 1802.

[L. S.] (Signed,) JUAN VENTURA MORALES.

By order of the Intendant.

(Signed,) CARLOS XIMENES.

Registered the foregoing title from page 41 to 43 of the book assigned for that purpose. New Orleans, 29th May, 1802.

(Signed,) XIMENES.

In the principal Comptroller's office the foregoing title has been registered in the book assigned for that purpose, at folio 10. New Orleans, 9th of June, 1802.

(Signed,) ARMIDEZ.

I, Don Carlos Trudeau, Surveyor Royal and Particular of the Province of Louisiana, andc., do certify, that in favor of, and in presence of (D. M. D.) and with the assistance of the syndic, Don Philip Sancier, and the adjoining neighbor, has been verified, bounded, and limited, a tract of land of one hundred and twenty-six arpens in front to the Bayou de los Lobos, with the ordinary depth of forty arpens, measured with the perche of the city of Paris, of eighteen feet long, measure of the said city; which tract of land is situated at the place called the Bay of St. Louis, on the southern bank of the Bayou de los Lobos; joining on the north part the bank of said bayou; on the south, land granted to Don F. S.; and on the other sides, by vacant lands of the domain of his Majesty, by parallel lines running southeast by south. On each limit has been planted a stake made of pine, driven into the ground to a depth of two feet; the first implanted upon the bank of the bayou, and the other at the foot of the high land; at the extremity of the ordinary forty arpens, I have planted no boundary, the soil being covered with water and impracticable, as it appears on the plan on the other side, which exhibits the extent and direction of the limits, andc. This survey has been made pursuant to a decree of his Lordship the Intendant-General, dated the 15th of the month of March last past. In testimony whereof, I have delivered these presents, with the foregoing figurative plan, the 15th of the month of April, 1802. Signed, I the present surveyor, and registered in the Book C, No. 3, fol. 62, at No. 1514, of the operations of survey.

I do certify that the present copy conforms to the original. Given to the interested party to enable him to proceed so as to obtain the corresponding title of grant in due form.

(Signed,) CARLOS TRUDEAU, Surveyor Royal.

This cause came on to be heard on the transcript of the record from the Circuit Court of the United States for the District of Missouri, and was argued by counsel. On consideration whereof, it is now here ordered and adjudged by this court, that the judgment of the said Circuit Court in this cause be, and the same is hereby, affirmed, with costs.

www.ingramcontent.com/pod-product-compliance
Lightning Source LLC
Chambersburg PA
CBHW070801180526
45168CB00004B/1703